Compiled by Angela R. Edwards

God's Love Fruit:
Walking Through the Fields of Grace and Mercy in Bloom

Compiled By:
Angela R. Edwards

Foreword By:
Marilyn E. Porter

Contributions By (in order of appearance):
Min. Aaron Weaver
CaTina Jenkins
Jayneiro Moore
Kisha Nicole
Laurie Benoit
Marlowe R. Scott
Natosha Lovall
Reyna Harris-Goynes
Shanericka Jones
Tosha Dearbone

Redemption's Story Publishing, LLC, Houston, Texas (USA)

God's Love Fruit

God's Love Fruit:
Walking Through the Fields of Grace and Mercy in Bloom

Copyright © 2019
Angela R. Edwards

All Rights Reserved.
No portion of this publication may be reproduced, stored in an electronic system, or transmitted in any form or by any means (electronic, mechanical, photocopy, recording, or otherwise) without written permission from the publisher. Brief quotations may be used in literary reviews.

Print ISBN 13: 978-1-947445-75-8
Digital ISBN 13: 978-1-947445-76-5
Library of Congress Control Number: 2019950788

Some names and identifying details have been changed to protect the privacy of individuals.

Scripture references are used with permission from Zondervan via Biblegateway.com.
Public Domain.

For information and bulk ordering, contact:
Redemption's Story Publishing, LLC
Angela Edwards, CEO
P.O. Box 62287
Houston, TX 77205
RedeemedByHim@Redemptions-Story.com

Compiled by Angela R. Edwards

Dedication

To anyone who has ever endured and overcame;
To those who choose to be loved and give love despite "the world" coming up against them:

This book is for YOU!

Acknowledgments

First and foremost, always giving honor and glory to the Holy Trinity: God the Father, God the Son, and God the Holy Spirit. Without Him, the gifts instilled in me would not blossom into all He has destined for them to be for His Kingdom.

To my very patient, loving, and supportive husband, **James Edwards**: Thank you for sacrificing some of "our time" while I work to build a legacy for our family. I love you!

To my children, **Anequilla Foots and Gerald Savage, III**: Mere words cannot express how grateful I am for the closeness of our relationship. As a young woman and man, you have endured more than any child should have, yet you never stopped loving me. I love you both!

To my mother, **Marlowe R. Scott**: You are appreciated **SO** much. I do my best to remind you of that fact at every turn. Thank you for being my second set of keen eyes! You are truly a *BLESSING* to me. Where would I be without your support? I love you, Mom!

To my bestie, **Marilyn E. Porter**: Time and again, you have shown **UP** and showed **OUT** on my behalf. Thank you for standing in my corner and for giving me gentle lifts when I felt weak. I am grateful to God for our 40+ years of friendship. I love you, Murl!

Compiled by Angela R. Edwards

To the host of **Contributing Authors** of *God's Love Fruit*: Thank you ALL for readily-agreeing to share your "Love Stories"! Neither of you hesitated to sow into the lives of the readers, and I, for one, appreciate you. My prayer is that your stories are life-changing for the masses. Amen and AMEN!

Last but not least, to every person who has had an influence on my life—whether positively or otherwise—I thank you as well. I would have no testimony without the tests nor a story without your impact.

Foreword

Marilyn E. Porter

Dedication:
This is dedicated to the ones who taught me how to love in every season of life.

Bio:
Marilyn E. Porter can be summed up in one word: Reflection. She is the mother of three biological daughters — a number that increases when spiritual daughters are added. She is a preaching and teaching woman with a strong Apostolic mantle on her shoulders. She is a businesswoman, which encompasses Christian Life and Integrity Coach, Professional Speaker, Best-Selling Author, Skilled Hybrid Publisher, and Business Consultant to both rising and seasoned entrepreneurs. Marilyn has the God-given ability to be the mirror that others often need to see the truth of God and themselves.

Compiled by Angela R. Edwards

"Love for All Seasons"

WINTER: When Love is Cold

Now, I already know that someone read that subtitle and thought, *"God is love, so love ain't ever cold!"* I won't deny that God is love; however, there are times in our lives (as humans) when God must allow us to learn by our own experiences — especially when we refuse to abide by His Word. That, my friend, can be a "cold season," yet God does, indeed, remain in a position of love.

The Winter season is often built on such things as pride, ego, rebellion, and repeated sin. Although we each have this tricky, little thing called "free will," God loves us way too much to allow us to feel good while we operate in our sin nature.

Brrrrrr...

Let's look at the Word:

Genesis 4:4-14, KJV

4 And Abel also brought an offering — fat portions from some of the firstborn of his flock. The LORD looked with favor on Abel and his offering,
5 but on Cain and his offering he did not look with favor. So, Cain was very angry, and his face was downcast.
6 Then the LORD said to Cain, "Why are you angry? Why is your face downcast?

God's Love Fruit

7 If you do what is right, will you not be accepted? But if you do not do what is right, sin is crouching at your door; it desires to have you, but you must rule over it."
8 Now Cain said to his brother Abel, "Let's go out to the field." While they were in the field, Cain attacked his brother Abel and killed him.
9 Then the Lord said to Cain, "Where is your brother Abel?"
"I don't know," he replied. "Am I my brother's keeper?"
10 The Lord said, "What have you done? Listen! Your brother's blood cries out to me from the ground.
11 Now you are under a curse and driven from the ground, which opened its mouth to receive your brother's blood from your hand.
12 When you work the ground, it will no longer yield its crops for you. You will be a restless wanderer on the earth."
13 Cain said to the Lord, "My punishment is more than I can bear.
14 Today you are driving me from the land, and I will be hidden from your presence; I will be a restless wanderer on the earth, and whoever finds me will kill me."

Cain's rebellion left him a banished wanderer. Can you say, ***"Now, that's cold!"***? If you are in a Winter season, may I suggest that you repent and seek God's face for access into a kinder, gentler season of His love? Don't hesitate!

Acts 3:19, KJV

19 Repent, then, and turn to God, so that your sins may be wiped out, that times of refreshing may come from the Lord…

Thank **GOD** that Winter doesn't last always!

Compiled by Angela R. Edwards

SPRING: When Love is Unpredictable

Spring is often a season of "one day to the next"—meaning, you are not sure if it's going to rain…so you always travel with an umbrella. Conversely, you are unsure if it will be 80 degrees or 45 degrees, so you dress with the possibility of both. What that looks like for me here in Georgia (where the weather is known to be a bit bipolar) is this: Old Navy jeans that look good with the legs rolled all the way down but also look good if I need to turn those jeans into pedal-pushers, a short-sleeve shirt with a light jacket or sweater than can be removed at about 68 degrees, and a pair of light tennis shoes that can be worn with or without thick ankle socks. You get the picture, right?

Springtime love leaves you unsure how you will show up in the world—while God yet loves you!

I call Springtime Love "The Season of Discernment-Sharpening." You must begin tapping into your God-connection more to get a jump on what lies ahead. In the onset of Spring, it's usually hit-or-miss, but as you draw closer to the next season, you have likely mastered the art of hearing the voice of God with precision.

It's a little chilly…

God's Love Fruit

Let's look at the Word:

1 Samuel 3:1-10, KJV

1 The boy Samuel ministered before the Lord under Eli. In those days, the word of the Lord was rare; there were not many visions.
2 One night, Eli, whose eyes were becoming so weak that he could barely see, was lying down in his usual place.
3 The lamp of God had not yet gone out, and Samuel was lying down in the house of the Lord, where the ark of God was.
4 Then the Lord called Samuel. Samuel answered, "Here I am."
5 And he ran to Eli and said, "Here I am; you called me." But Eli said, "I did not call; go back and lie down." So, he went and lay down.
6 Again the Lord called, "Samuel!" And Samuel got up and went to Eli and said, "Here I am; you called me." "My son," Eli said, "I did not call; go back and lie down."
7 Now Samuel did not yet know the Lord: The word of the Lord had not yet been revealed to him.
8 A third time the Lord called, "Samuel!" And Samuel got up and went to Eli and said, "Here I am; you called me." Then Eli realized that the Lord was calling the boy.
9 So Eli told Samuel, "Go and lie down, and if he calls you, say, 'Speak, Lord, for your servant is listening.'" So Samuel went and lay down in his place.
10 The Lord came and stood there, calling as at the other times, "Samuel! Samuel!" Then Samuel said, "Speak, for your servant is listening."

SUMMER: When Love is Hot

Summertime love is hot, hot, **HOT**! The anointing of God is upon you, and you are walking that walk and talking that talk. Nothing can come between you and your Lover. His hand is on you and can't nobody tell you a thing!

Summer is a season of power and positioning. It's also the season where the Winter culprits will try to rear their ugly heads. You guessed it correctly if you said, *"The pride of power and position can interrupt Summer love…if we're not careful."* We cannot forget that even when it's hot, we must stay submitted and surrendered to the will of God for our lives.

Summer love requires daily doses of silence before your Lover. He needs your attention like never before to keep the fire (anointing) burning deep within you. Summer love draws you in so deep, and you have to remember to care for the people in your life. Summer love will get you caught up, so remember to be mindful of the mere earthling in your life (husband/wife, children, parents, friends, church members, etc.). I know it's hot and heavy, but be careful not to burn out on passion. Let us remember that seasons change, and so that we might not faint when this Summer love balances out, hold fast to the fact that everything here is just for a season.

Some like it HOT…

Let's look at the Word:

Ecclesiastes 3:1-11, KJV

1 To everything there is a season, and a time to every purpose under the heaven:
2 A time to be born, and a time to die; a time to plant, and a time to pluck up that which is planted;
3 A time to kill, and a time to heal; a time to break down, and a time to build up;
4 A time to weep, and a time to laugh; a time to mourn, and a time to dance;
5 A time to cast away stones, and a time to gather stones together; a time to embrace, and a time to refrain from embracing;
6 A time to get, and a time to lose; a time to keep, and a time to cast away;
7 A time to rend, and a time to sew; a time to keep silence, and a time to speak;
8 A time to love, and a time to hate; a time of war, and a time of peace.
9 What profit hath he that worketh in that wherein he laboureth?
10 I have seen the travail, which God hath given to the sons of men to be exercised in it.
11 He hath made everything beautiful in his time: he hath set the world in their heart, so that no man can find out the work that God maketh from the beginning to the end.

Compiled by Angela R. Edwards

FALL: When Love Rejuvenates

Do you love pancakes as much as I do? It's my favorite breakfast food of all time, but not without butter and some sweet mapley syrup. Now, I don't quite know if "mapley" is a word, but it sounds better than maple-like—a sort of pseudo maple syrup. Okay. Simply put: I like the faint taste of maple, but not quite the real thing.

Anyhow, the whole mention of maple syrup is to note that the sap that generates the syrup is manufactured from a seemingly dead tree! Yes, when the leaves are gone, and the bark looks dry…when the tree is outwardly resting—God is producing that sweet maple flavor.

The Fall love is a season of simply resting in the Father as He revives and rejuvenates you.

I am a Fall baby. I was born amid the crisp air of Thanksgiving Eve in 1969. I am a bit partial to the season of rest for all of nature, yet it is the toughest season for me to endure because I struggle with the "nothingness" of these times in my life. Still, God is so gracious that He prompted me to learn about the maple tree's season of mass production, which is during a time of rest.

I want to encourage you to receive the blessing of scheduled rest. Today, I fully embrace Fall love as my Sabbath season.

Rest is good for the soul…

Let's look at the Word:

Mark 2:27, KJV

27 Then he said to them, "The Sabbath was made for man, not man for the Sabbath."

Love is **always** around in some form. God knows the season, and He knows the modality in which you need to be loved. God knows your love language and is speaking it to you in *EVERY* season!

Compiled by Angela R. Edwards

The following Spirit-inspired poem was gifted to Marlowe Scott for this literary work in August 2019. It is shared here with you as yet another way to express **GOD'S LOVE**:

One of a Kind Love — A Poem
© 2019 Marlowe R. Scott

Love is an endearing, special word
Interpreted in numerous spoken and unspoken ways.
The scriptures tell of God's love in action,
As He leads and guide us along life's days.

We find human love in parents who may sacrifice
To give their family food, shelter, and clothes.
How much more our loving God supplies
With the many unmerited blessings He bestows!

Our loving God is not like those here on Earth.
They may hurt, disappoint, and betray.
When we displease God, He forgives and forgets our trespasses.
As His children, God's LOVE is our greatest mainstay!

Peace, joy, and protection we have
From dangers seen and unseen of all kind.
Our God will never leave us in our struggles;
He's ready to comfort and is the GREATEST LOVE we'll ever find!

Introduction

When you think of the word "LOVE," what images come to mind? Do you envision walking along the shoreline, holding hands with your significant other? Perhaps your definition of love is planted on the surface, as you consider those things you can see and touch. Maybe your definition involves the protection and sacrifice expected of both yourself and others, especially the parental figures in your life. There is no right or wrong way to define the expression of love, as it varies from one person to the next and can easily be justified as the primary source of "feeling."

However, there is a biblical account of 'LOVE' unlike any other that is said in the following manner:

"Love is patient, love is kind. It does not envy, it does not boast, it is not proud. It does not dishonor others, it is not self-seeking, it is not easily angered, it keeps no record of wrongs. Love does not delight in evil but rejoices with the truth. It always protects, always trusts, always hopes, always perseveres" **(1 Corinthians 13:4-7, NIV).**

In *God's Love Fruit: Walking the Fields of Grace and Mercy in Bloom*, each story shared speaks of disappointments and pains that were, in some way, meant to hinder and discourage the author. The Holy Bible says the enemy of our soul — Satan — comes to steal, kill, and destroy, and he was hot on the heels of each writer while working vehemently to gain their souls for his kingdom in Hell.

OH, BUT GOD!

Although we, in our flawed humanness, may attempt to do "it" all on our own, God is always there—watching, waiting, and at the ready to receive us back into His loving arms…when we acknowledge we need **HIM** to work "it" out. In the Old Testament, He speaks to us through the Prophet Isaiah in this way:

"Therefore, the LORD longs to be gracious to you, and therefore He waits on high to have compassion on you. For the LORD is a God of justice; how blessed are all those who long for Him" **(Isaiah 30:18, NASB).**

There will be difficult times…**BUT GOD!**

There will be moments of disappointment in humanity…**BUT GOD!**

Your family and friends may turn their backs on you…**BUT GOD!**

You may want to throw in the towel and end it all…**BUT GOD!**

Indeed, as the scripture says, we are **BLESSED!** As each contributor to this project penned his or her truth, they set aside those feelings of rejection and judgment to sow into *YOUR* soul. In 2,000 words or less, they poured out their hearts to assure *YOU* that there is hope for tomorrow. You are encouraged to never give up on your journey.

Don't allow the enemy to win. The devil has a secured fate: to burn in Hell for all of eternity. Conversely, we have a choice—to join him **OR** spend eternity in Heaven with streets that are paved with gold and while Heavenly angels glorify God all the day long. **NOW** is your time to show Satan that you

God's Love Fruit

KNOW you are loved by an awesome and forgiving God! You may have gone through the fire, but you are promised in God's Word to come out on the other side without so much as the scent of smoke!

Glory! Hallelujah! Stand up and take your place in God's Kingdom!

Compiled by Angela R. Edwards

"Love the Lord your God with all your heart and with all your soul and with all your mind and with all your strength. The second is this: 'Love your neighbor as yourself.' There is no commandment greater than these."

(Mark 12:30-31, NIV)

Table of Contents

Dedication vi
Acknowledgments vii
Foreword —Marilyn E. Porter ix
   "Love for All Seasons" x
One of a Kind Love — A Poem xviii
Introduction xix
Min. Aaron Weaver 1
   "Love, Honor, and Obey" 2
Angela R. Edwards 6
   "Love Lost: Self-Love Found" 7
CaTina Jenkins 14
   "Don't Forget About Me: The Visit" 15
Jayneiro Moore 17
   "Why Didn't He Love Me?" 18
Kisha Nicole 24
   "WHY Do I Have to Love THEM?" 25
Laurie Benoit 32
   "A Not-So-Simple Love Story" 33
Marlowe R. Scott 41
   "No Greater Love" 42
Natosha Lovall 48
   "To Love and Be Loved…God's Way" 49
Reyna Harris-Goynes 55
   "With Pain Comes Strength and Love" 56

Compiled by Angela R. Edwards

Shanericka Jones 63
   "Just Call Me 'Self-Control'" 64
Tosha Dearbone 69
   "Love Wins!" 70
Conclusion: God's Love is for ALL 77
Tell God ALL about it! 79
About the Compiler 83
Contact the Publisher 86

Min. Aaron Weaver

Dedication:

This is dedicated to God **ALMIGHTY**. I'm grateful for Him bringing me through many storms in my life. I also dedicate this to the memory of my wife, Verda, who went home to be with the LORD in 2014, after 19 years of marriage.

Bio:

Min. Aaron Weaver is on the ministerial staff at New Life Worship and Praise Center in Amite, Louisiana, under the leadership of Pastor Johnnie L. Tamez. Through his studies at Union Theological Seminary and other institutions, he has embraced deliverance as his calling. He is the Best-Selling Author of the book *I Once Was Blind, But Now I See*—a piece of literary art that is sure to open your eyes and have you referring to it time and again.

Compiled by Angela R. Edwards

"Love, Honor, and Obey"

L**ove. Honor. Obey.** Many people think those words are only applicable to marriage. However, before we can learn how to serve, we must acknowledge that they also apply to one's commitment in **any** relationship—especially between a husband and wife.

How can we say we love that special person in our life if we don't know God?

To learn and know how to love, honor, and obey one another, those things must first be taught in the home. For those who have rarely been shown or had love expressed openly in the home, the differences are clearly evident.

Take, for example, the tainted love associated with fornication (sex before/outside of marriage). A woman may have sex with one man or many men just to get hold of their money so that he can take care of her. Perhaps that same woman purposely had children with different men and, when the relationships don't work out, she must prostitute herself to get the monies needed to care for her children. The point I'm making here is this: She would rather serve Satan by catering to her physical needs, instead of relying on God Almighty to supply her every need. It's up to you whether you will allow the demons to rule and reign in your life.

Proverbs 3:5-7 says that God will permit the enemy to attack you. The purpose is to strengthen your faith as you learn to trust in God and not depend on yourself.

If you're one of the people who say, *"I'm grown. I go where I want. I sleep with whomever I wish. This is my body. I will do with it what I will,"* then you must know this: That's **NOT** your body. God made that body for you to live in. You, my dear, are a *spirit*. If the former is your choice of lifestyle, then you're already living for Satan. Doing so is the equivalent of participating in voodoo, witchcraft, lying, stealing, murdering, abortions, and a host of other sins. Point blank, you are doing Satan's will (serving him), and he gladly will keep you bound in those chains! **Remember always: Satan comes to kill, steal, and destroy.**

Are you going to let him reign in your life and rob you of your victory? The choice is yours. If you have yet to accept Jesus Christ as your personal Savior, your soul is bound for the Lake of Fire to **burn forever** with your tempter, Satan. You are in direct opposition of God if you do not repent. Ask yourself this question: Is it worth burning for all of eternity in a place where money, jewelry, designer shoes and clothes, your house, and fancy car will do you no good?

To those men who prostitute their women, that's not love. Rest assured God will hold you accountable. Your job is to help bring out the woman of God that's inside of her. You are also responsible for helping her keep her body pure until marriage. In turn, you will become a man of God—a mature man, a wise husband, and proficient leader.

Men, love your girlfriend/wife with the love of God. Don't look at her as merely a sex object and then break up when you've "finished" with her, just for her to turn around and become another man's whore. **That is not love.**

If God is not in your heart, and you have not renewed your mind by accepting Jesus Christ as your Savior, your soul will remain eternally lost.

Humanity gives the title "Love" to situations that God calls abominations, such as:

- Shacking up
- Committing adultery
- Fornication
- Men having sex with men and marrying each other
- Women having sex with women and marrying each other

Those things have been accepted by man, but it was not and never will be accepted by GOD!

Genesis 19:24 states, *"And the LORD rained upon Sodom and Gomorrah, brimstone and fire from the LORD from the heavens."* That action was in direct response to humanity's acceptance of forbidden "love."

You are encouraged to read Proverbs 6:16-19, where it discusses six things that God hates, and seven that are an abomination to Him.

When we put and keep on the whole armor of God (Ephesians 6:10-18), our problems are lessened, and we have more victories in Jesus' name! Read it for yourself and see who your real enemy is—one who does not know love...the enemy of our soul.

GOD loved us so much, He made us in His image (see Genesis 1:28).

God's Love Fruit

GOD loved us before the foundation of the world (see Ephesians 1:14).

GOD so loves us, that He gave us His Son (see John 3:16).

GOD said obedience is better than sacrifice (see Jeremiah 7:21).

Love is serving God by serving others. True love will say no to what is wrong and not continuously compromise their love for others for their love for God. **THAT** is love!

Compiled by Angela R. Edwards

Angela R. Edwards

Dedication:
My story is dedicated to my children, Anequilla and Gerald, for their steadfast love despite my choices in the past.

Bio:
Angela R. Edwards is a wife, mother, grandmother, daughter, a woman of God, and CEO of Pearly Gates Publishing and Redemption's Story Publishing. A New Jersey native now residing in Houston, Texas, she has embraced the southern culture in its fullness while never straying far from her northern roots. She is the visionary behind the *"God's Fruit"* redemptive series of books and believes every man, woman, and youth has a story to tell. Angela's business motto is: *"Your words have POWER!"* — and works to that end to provide affordable and all-inclusive publishing services to both new and seasoned authors.

"Love Lost: Self-Love Found"

"**H**URRY! PACK IT ALL UP BEFORE HE GETS BACK!" Those were the words spoken by me, not one...not two...but three times during the tumultuous relationship with a man I should have left long before instance number one.

Unlike some others, I was not experiencing "daddy issues." As a matter of fact, my father and I had a solid and loving father/daughter relationship that was despised by some. To further prove my point, my father actually helped with instances two and three!

So, you might be wondering, *"What was she running from?"* I was attempting to flee a relationship with a man who was an irresponsible crack addict. I was soul-tied to a man who had the devil riding his back like a surfer "riding the wave," refusing to fall. Admittedly, I loved that man very much. For over seven years, on and off, I gave him chance after chance to get his life in order. Much to my chagrin, he didn't get the message that I was done with "trying to fix him."

The decisions for my children and me to pack up and relocate in his absence weren't made lightly. Although we never moved far away, just the thought of him returning to an empty home brought me some sense of peace. I hated that my children were subjected to the lack of parenting on his behalf. No, they weren't his "responsibility"; they were mine and always have been. However, as it is with blended families, as the adults in the relationship, we should come together and fulfill the roles as "mother and father." He failed miserably. I do, however, accept my level of fault. I didn't insist he stand and do what was necessary to ensure my children had a positive male role model in their lives. I chose to endure, hope…and love.

The first time we packed up and moved, I had already secured a new home for my children and me. It was about five blocks away from the house we lived in when he and first met—the one he made "his home" roughly eight months into our relationship. At the time, I had no idea when he would return, as he was out on one of his crack binges and could opt to come back at any moment. Still, I was sure he wouldn't make his reappearance anytime soon because he was often gone for days at a time.

Just as my children and I were getting settled in (about four days after the move), sure enough, he returned…to an empty house. I recall purposefully leaving the window shades up inside so that when he came back, he didn't even have to turn the doorknob to know we were gone. Spiteful, I know. Nonetheless, I felt he deserved the hopeless feeling I'm sure he experienced. What I didn't expect was my old neighbors telling him where we were.

When the knock came at the door, it was him on the other side. He cried (literally), begged (loudly), and made promise after promise (emptily) that he would change. He went on to say he knew he was wrong and that he understood I didn't deserve his mistreatment and lack of concern for the family unit. I didn't immediately take him back, though. I sent him on his way, back to his parents' house. He stayed there for roughly two weeks, all while calling me daily and professing his love for me. After enduring feeling lonely for those couple of weeks, I allowed him back into our lives.

I saw a change in him, which gave me hope that my tactic had, indeed, worked! He found a new job, worked hard, and brought his paychecks home. What a welcome gesture it was in light of the past where he would get a job, work until he earned his first check, and then go out binging on his addiction—eventually coming home penniless. Life was good for some time before addiction reared its ugly head again, prompting me to throw in the towel and make preparations for my children and me to move yet again.

I don't know why, but I thought that moving was easier than facing him and telling him *HE* had to go.

THE CYCLE CONTINUES...

Time number two came about when he "borrowed" my son's bike late one night and, when he returned the following morning, he was on foot. I was **LIVID**! It was one thing to hurt and disappointment me, but don't mess with my children! The mother bear in me tore into him, and I knew at that moment, there was no hope for our relationship. He had crossed the line! Immediately after that instance, he reverted to his old ways, which gave me just the push I needed to begin prepping to relocate again.

I called my father, explained to him all that was going on (conveniently leaving out the part about the addiction), and asked him to help me find a house where "my love" couldn't find me. I was pleased to learn there was an available apartment right down the street from my father, so I met with the landlord and signed the lease on the spot.

Although I was sick and tired of the inconvenience of feeling as if running was the best option, I was hopeful that *THIS* move would bring me the serenity I longed for. There was **NO** way he could find me because I wasn't telling **ANYONE** we had in common where we were going.

I failed to factor in my children's desire to stay connected to their friends. You guessed correctly if you said, *"He found you…and you took him back."* I won't go into all the details here, but know that his begging and pleading were relentless. That time, however, I held out for a few months. I wanted to see for myself if the change he said he made would last. Once I felt sure he was on the right track and had, indeed, gotten himself clean, I took him back. By that time, our relationship was well into our fifth year of on-again/off-again teeter-tottering.

And so, the cycle repeated. All was well. All went sour. My children and I moved one last time, back to our "hometown" where it all began.

Yes, he found us (my doing that time). Yes, he attempted to get his life in order. Yes, he failed miserably. Yes, I still loved him. Yes, I had **FINALLY** reached my end.

I refused to uproot my children again on account of "some man." The light had shone brightly on what my decisions were doing to them. **I WAS DONE!** I stood up to him and told him he had to *GO!* Of course, due to the past, he was sure I was "just mad" and that he would be back in my good graces soon enough.

GOD'S REVELATION

Every day that ticked by, I learned the healing power of prayer. I prayed for the soul-tie to be broken. I prayed for peace. I prayed for my children. I even prayed for him. As time progressed, I found myself being strengthened. I asked God to show me why I allowed myself to be mistreated for so long. What He showed me shocked me!

As confident in myself as I believed I was, I was dealing with low self-esteem.

Wow! That was quite the revelation! I had to dig deep to figure out where I had "gone wrong." As I began to reflect on my life up to that point, I thought back to my failed marriage (the relationship before "him"). In that relationship, I was mentally, emotionally, and physically abused. It was determined that I embraced the mistreatment by "him" because he "only emotionally abused me." Idiotic way of thinking, I know. As I stated, I held out hope that he could and would change his ways. I donned my strong mask and believed that he — a preacher's kid — knew what he was doing to himself and me was wrong. After all, wasn't I worth him getting it right?

Here's the thing that God taught me through those seven years: Only HE can change people when He wants and how He wants. All of the running away I did while calling myself "teaching him a lesson" was in error. In no way would God get the glory for a change made in my then-mate if I continued to tolerate the mess of a life he had made for himself…and my family. Was I trying to take the place of God by trying to enforce change?

Guilty as charged.

I'm sorry, God.

God's Word often speaks of the sanctification process. One way is in **Psalm 1:1-3 (NIV)** —

"Blessed is the one who does not walk in step with the wicked or stand in the way that sinners take or sit in the company of mockers, but whose delight is in the law of the Lord and who meditates on His law day and night. That person is like a tree planted by streams of water, which yields its fruit in season and whose leaf does not wither — whatever they do prospers."

In essence, time and again, I expected a quick change in that man's life, but that's not God's way. **GOD** is methodical and works in and through our lives in His perfect time.

RESULTS AND BLESSINGS

Today, I operate from a place of knowing *AND* freedom. After getting my own life in order and focusing exclusively on what it was that God had for **ME**, I met, fell in love with, and married a man who's **not** emotionally, mentally, or physically abusive. His name is James, and we've been married for 12 years (at the time of this writing).

I went through the "FIRE" for seven years and came out virtually unscathed, giving **ALL** glory to God for His lovingkindness, grace, and mercy. The love I lost opened the door to the love I found. I am in a much better place, with my issues of low self-esteem being a thing of the distant past.

In closing, you are encouraged to do your own self-assessment. Seek God's guidance in ALL things, especially as it directly relates to your spiritual health. We all have moments of weakness in this journey called "Life." It is then that we must lean on God for strength, deliverance, and a *LOVE* unlike any other.

Ephesians 2:4-5 (NIV) —

"But because of His great love for us, God, who is rich in mercy, made us alive with Christ, even when we were dead in transgressions. It is by His grace we are saved."

Compiled by Angela R. Edwards

CaTina Jenkins

Dedication:
To my wonderful five children: Jaelyn, Caitlin, Josiah, Tamoriona, and Ty'Aveia. You can do all things through Christ who strengthens you (Philippians 4:13)! I Love You!

Bio:
CaTina Jenkins is a new author and Mentor for teenage girls with Positive Express based out of Houston, Texas. A Shreveport, Louisiana native, she was raised in the small town of Homer where she graduated from Homer High School. From there, she continued her educational pursuit by attending college. CaTina is the mother of five children; three biological (Jaelyn, Caitlin, and Josiah). She also adopted her two nieces (Tamoriona and Ty'Aveia). She attends The Fountain of Praise in Houston, Texas, under the leadership of Pastor Remus E. Wright.

"Don't Forget About Me: The Visit"

As Chyna sat across from Gee Money during one of their rare opportunities to spend time together due to her hectic work schedule, she looked at him with adoration, love, and white-hot passion in her eyes. It was as if everything she had ever lost came back to her when she was with him: her joy, love, inner strength, power, and a genuine smile. Chyna could not deny that he added value to her life. Whenever she needed that extra push to make it through to another day, Gee Money was right there—motivating and inspiring her to be better and to go after her dreams and goals. Without a doubt, he was her biggest supporter.

Often, no words needed to be spoken between the two of them. Chyna could tell, just by the look in Gee Money's eyes, that he needed her as much as she needed him. His bright smile relayed the message loud and clear: "I love you, Chyna." Although they were soon to part ways, Chyna constantly reassured Gee Money that he was everything she needed and more. By far, he was the most handsome man she had ever seen; a caramel complexion, jet black hair, perfect white teeth, tall, and muscular. He was so sexy and definitely easy on the eyes.

Gee Money had a way of making love to Chyna without a sexual encounter. His city accent and strong, authoritative demeanor turned her all the way on. She couldn't keep her eyes off him and loved to just listen to him talk. He intrigued her as she hung onto his every word. He was a man who described himself as a gangster but a gentleman with class. Oh, yes: He was definitely the latter! The chemistry between the two of them was remarkable and undeniable, as if they had known each other for years.

With everything in him, Gee Money loved Chyna and wished he could do so much more for the woman God placed in his life. It was his heart's desire to give her the world, but with the threat of his long-term incarceration looming, he began to feel as if he was holding Chyna back from being with someone who could, indeed, give her everything she both needed and deserved…those things he could not provide for her at that time.

Without a doubt, Chyna was in love with a man who was perfect for her, despite his current "situation." She could envision a future with him and vowed to love him through everything he endured, even committing herself only to him.

After eating breakfast, the time came for Chyna to end the visit and return home; however, she promised Gee Money she would return on her next weekend off from work. She hated having to leave, as with each visit, they grew closer and closer together. It was evident love was in the air and that the feelings were mutual.

Once she returned home, the two of them continued their routine of talking on the phone every morning and every night before they went to bed. All the while, Gee Money continued to make love to Chyna's mind with every word he spoke. She knew early on in their relationship that she couldn't approach him with her physical needs; she had to do so in prayer. After all, he often reminded her of what the scripture says: *"Therefore, what God has joined together, let not man separate"* **(Mark 10:9, NKJV).**

Jayneiro Moore

Dedication:
This snippet of my story is dedicated to all the men who had to grow up without a father. I pray peace and closure for you, just as I now have.

Bio:
Jayneiro D. Moore, Sr., a New York native, is a professional Commercial Truck Driver and Hazmat Specialist at Republic Energy and Industrial Services. He counsels those who are dealing with serious life and marital issues. He has a unique counseling style, in that he uses the Word of God for empowerment and a bit of comedy for uplifting. Jayneiro spends his free time bowling, watching sports, going to the gun range, and spending time with his family. Mr. Moore has been happily married to Kisha Nicole for the last 17 years, and they have five awesome children together.

"Why Didn't He Love Me?"

As far back as I can recall, I was born into *trauma*. As it was told to me by my dad, when my mom first gave birth to me, he was not there. His reason was that he and my mom hit a rough patch, and he was unsure that I was his child. I know that my parents were married, but I have no recollection of them being together.

I remember my mom struggling to support me by herself.

I also remember my dad popping up every couple of years to see my brother and me.

The sad thing is that he lived a couple of towns over from us on Long Island, New York — approximately 20 minutes away. It wasn't as if he lived in another state! When a child knows he has a father, but the father refuses to come around, it really confuses the child. I often wondered, *"Is something wrong with me? Is it something I did? Does he love me?"*

At the age of seven, I found out the real reason why my father neglected us: he fell victim to the '80s crack epidemic. I recall my dad coming to visit my brother and me when I was around eight years old. At the time, he had a Caucasian woman with him — and my mother went **ballistic**! To her, it was a slap in the face. I didn't see my father again until I was 11.

Whenever my dad did come around, he would use the typical excuse that the young boys use nowadays: *"I would come around more often, but your mother is crazy and always trying to have me locked up."* **That was a lie.** Even though I was young, I was sharp enough to know my dad chose to smoke crack, rather than to be a father to me and show me how to be a man. (I suppose it's hard to show someone how to be a man when you're not a man yourself.)

Strangely, my dad grew up with both his parents and several siblings. As far as I know, my grandfather was there for him. I used to think, *"How **DARE** you grow up with a father and not take care of your **own** seeds!"*

My mom did the best she could as a single parent, and I was a well-behaved child…until I became a teenager. My mom worked a lot of doubles trying to provide for me by herself with no financial support from my father. The last time he gave my mother any money was when I was in the 8th grade, and that money was for school shopping. He gave her $100.00 and acted like he really did something amazing.

Throughout my adolescent and teenage years, I built up resentment and hatred for my father, although I still loved him. I couldn't understand how I could love someone who didn't seem to love me in return. By the time I turned 16, I had started being mischievous, which led me to my first time being incarcerated. Now, I'm not going to say that if my father had been in my life more, I would've been an angel. I will, however, say I might not have gotten into trouble so much. I ended up getting locked up three more times, with the fourth time landing me in the penitentiary. At the age of 18, I was locked away in the Elmira Correctional Facility. (Ironically, my dad did time in the same prison when he was 18.)

While in prison, my father wrote me **one** letter. When I came home after being released at the age of 20, I started to see my father more often and tried to build a relationship with him. Unfortunately, I couldn't seem to get over the fact that he wasn't there for me when I needed him. Once I started having children of my own, my hatred for him grew. I have three sons out of five children and have always been there for them.

Throughout the years, my father had the audacity to try to make me feel guilty about not visiting him. ***Can you believe that?*** I felt that with him being the parent, **he** should have made more attempts to check on me versus **me** going to check on him. When I got older and started driving, I visited him once in a blue moon. I even did some asphalt work with him. That situation didn't go so well. It's hard to work with someone whose sole purpose is to work fast, just to get off and smoke crack. He would talk to me about getting off work and going to get a hit, which really pissed me off! How dare he! I would think, *"I can't believe this dude is telling me that when he gets off work, he's going to get himself one!"* I don't think he realized I knew that was the reason I was neglected.

Even though my brother was neglected as well, my father showed more favoritism towards him than me. Later, he would tell me that I'm smarter and stronger than my older brother. That may be true, but I still wished he would have been there for me. I don't know if anyone else who has a deadbeat dad ever felt that way, but the more I went to Parent/Teacher Night, had lunch with my children at school, took road trips with my wife and children, attended my children's sporting events, took them shopping, cut my sons' hair, and just did those things a father is supposed to do for his family, the more I hated him.

Once I got in my late 20s and early 30s, I would make the phone conversations between my father and me very short. He would try to give me fatherly advice, and I would dismiss him. I knew I was wrong, but I didn't care. I was "in my feelings." I knew at one point, I had to forgive him because I didn't want to block my blessings. By the time I hit my mid-thirties, I had let the hate I had towards my father disrupt my personal life. I know my wife and children took notice of my negative behavior patterns. I believe I displayed so much hate for him because deep down inside, I loved him.

It's funny how I could love someone who didn't love me back. My wife suggested I get counseling to deal with my issues regarding my father. In my stubbornness—a trait many men carry—I would respond, *"I don't need no damn counseling!"* I remained in denial until I finally listened to my wife and scheduled an appointment with a counselor.

The first session with the counselor, I wasn't very transparent. However, each time I went, I opened more. By the time my fourth visit came, I felt like a new man! My wife could see the difference as well. After a while, I stopped going to counseling because I thought I was healed...but I wasn't.

My father would call me, and I wouldn't answer the phone—the reason why was because I was not in the right state of mind to speak to him. I would have been extremely rude and disrespectful. Scripture says, *"Honor your father and your mother, so that your days may be long in the land that the Lord your God gives you"* (Exodus 20:12). For about a year, my father made several attempts to reach me. My wife suggested I answer the phone, talk to him, and let him know how I felt. I was very stubborn, prideful, and hardheaded, so I wasn't trying to hear what she said.

My father finally got tired of calling and me not answering. I then chose to call him, and he was shocked! He asked me, *"Why didn't you answer the phone when I called?"* He then pointedly asked, **"What did I ever do, son?"**

That was my opened door! *"It's not what you did; it's what you **didn't** do,"* I replied.

My father is extremely "old school," and his thought-process is like talking to someone who's mentality is stuck in the '60s. To make a long story short, he never admitted to the fact that he was not there for me because of his drug addiction. All I was looking for was an apology, which I never received.

It was not until I relocated to Texas in November 2013 that I realized the following: Sometimes, when people — especially relatives — do you wrong, you must accept the fact that you may never get an apology. It's okay, though. The fact that they didn't apologize is not your fault.

My wife took a counseling course to become a Certified Christian Counselor. Every day when she came home, she was excited and told me how the course was helping her with things she and her classmates were dealing with. That piqued my interest and had me considering taking the course as well. She also told me about how great her instructor was. In January 2017, my wife graduated, and I met her instructor, Dr. Alice Millsap. When I met her, and my wife informed her I would be taking the course, Dr. Millsap's spirit and energy were nothing like I have ever felt before. My wife specifically told her, *"I want my husband to be in **your** class."*

In August 2017, I began the 16-week course. All throughout, Dr. Millsap helped me realize I had some healing to do before I could counsel others. I was going through some tough times in my life at the time and had lost my job. Dr. Millsap prayed for me that I would find another job, and within two weeks, I was reemployed. At one point, I found myself wanting to give up on the course due to unresolved issues pertaining to my father. Dr. Millsap convinced me to keep on pushing and encourage me by saying, *"You are almost there."* Her prayers and the support from the rest of the class and my family were what motivated me to finish. She also told me that I had to forgive my father in order to move on.

I did not want to call him and forgive him, but I knew it was **necessary** if I wanted to move on and be successful in life. I finally called him up and forgave him. He then apologized and told me I was a better man and father than he could have ever been. That apology and acknowledgment were all I was seeking. I now speak to my father at least once a week, and we talk about work and football.

This experience has taught me the value of forgiveness and extending second chances to others. I pray that others will follow in my footsteps and forgive, relieving themselves of the burden that unforgiveness can produce.

Compiled by Angela R. Edwards

Kisha Nicole

Dedication:
This excerpt of my story is dedicated to my oldest son Robert. There's nothing on this earth that can separate you and I. You're stuck with me! I love you **ALWAYS**!

Bio:
Servant. Wife. Mother. Counselor. Coach. Creative. Kisha Nicole, a New York native, is a professional Embellisher, Christian Counselor, Mental Health Peer Specialist, and Recovery Support Peer Specialist. Some of her hobbies include crafting, baking, makeup artistry, sewing, and decorating. In addition to her creative talents, she has a heart for the things of God, and her goal is to see all of God's children healed, delivered, and set free. This proud graduate of Georgia State University has been married to Jayneiro D. Moore, Sr. for 17 years, and they have five awesome children.

"WHY Do I Have to Love THEM?"

The date was Sunday, August 31, 2014—the day my oldest and middle sons (ages 16 and 12 respectively) decided to run away from home. My husband and I didn't even know they were gone until our youngest daughter came into our room and asked, *"Where are the boys?"* Although she had asked a question, she inadvertently informed us they weren't in the house. After searching thoroughly from room to room, we realized that they, in fact, had left with their bookbags filled with clothes. We then called the police to report them missing…and to protect ourselves as parents.

It must be noted here that my oldest son's rebellious nature was nothing new. He'd been caught skipping school and smoking weed—all while hanging out with the wrong crowds. Regarding his truancy, his actions had put my husband's and my driver's licenses in jeopardy **AND** put us all at risk of receiving a $500.00 fine. Yup, you read that right: **$1,500.00 in penalties for the three of us!** I can't fail to mention that my husband, Jay, has a Commercial Driver's License with all endorsements, so that would have really messed him up.

When the police came, they took the report and filed a missing person's report for both boys. Later that same evening, my middle son returned home on his own. As for my oldest son, we didn't know at the time that it would be two years before we would lay eyes on him again.

You see, my oldest son had **ALWAYS** been defiant and rambunctious in his youth. He stayed in so much trouble while in elementary school, he was placed in special education classes because *'THEY'* said he had ADHD. Now, I will be the first to admit my son is unique—just as I am! Isn't that how God made us? Aren't we all His individual, hand-sculpted creations? I've never seen ADHD, Autism, Dyslexia, or any of those other "labels" in the Bible when God describes His creations. As such, I've always had trouble subscribing to those diagnoses. Thinking back on it, the devil had been trying to take my son out since he was five years old! (I would later come to realize my son had a Prophetic Call on his life that's so huge, the enemy would stop at nothing to kill him.)

Conversely, my son could also be the sweetest, most thoughtful, and helpful child you'd ever encounter.

During the two years he was gone, I endured some of the most heart-wrenching pain and torment a person—**A MOTHER**—could ever experience. Now, there were several times my son called me, yet I had **NO** idea where *exactly* he was. At every turn, he led me to believe he was still in the Houston, Texas area "living with people." I took and held onto that information while fervently praying and believing for his return.

I remember the very first conversation we had after he left. At the time, I was driving to Bible study. During the call, my child spoke to me in a way in which I **KNEW** the devil was operating in his life. He told me I wouldn't amount to anything and that my business was a failure. I specifically recall him saying, *"Oh, yeah. You're supposed to be an entrepreneur, right? But you ain't sold nothing but ten t-shirts in all these years, huh? Hahahahahaha!"* That laughter was disgustingly piercing to my ears. I was so hurt by his words. After all, he was the one I spent the most time with because I homeschooled him during his middle school years. He accompanied me to all my vendor events and was very helpful during that time. For him to know all I'd been working towards and then say that to me? It literally felt like those words were concrete boulders falling on me!

It was **GOD** who reminded me that it wasn't **REALLY** my son speaking; rather, it was a demonic spirit.

I ended up hanging up on my son, which only served to add to my pain!

Now, during that time, everyone acted as if they had no idea where my son was. I had limited conversations with my oldest daughter, who was living in Atlanta, Georgia, with my mom, dad, and two sisters (my relationships with them have **ALWAYS** been rocky). See, I'm the rebellious one who goes against the grain and refuses to be controlled by *ANYONE!* I am what people often refer to as the classic "black sheep in the family." I'm the one who says and does everything most others won't. LOL! Hey, I wear that crown proudly…thank you very much!

Truthfully, God sent me to Houston to get *away* from my family because of what He wanted to do in me and my life.

Back to my son…

During the period when he was gone, there were many incidents of teen violence and criminal activity occurring regularly. You know how the news always gives the bad news first? I used to watch the news daily, praying my son's image wouldn't be plastered on the TV screen. Every time his picture wasn't "Breaking News," I would breathe a **HUGE** sigh of relief! I would think, *"Okay. He's **probably** not dead,"* and that gave me hope…until the next day and the next. The overwhelming feeling of fear gripped my heart every single day he was gone. **UGH!!!**

So, as I've said, my son called me a few times while he was away from home. As time progressed, our conversations got better, but I was still under the impression he was close to home. I remember when we moved into our second rental house in 2015, he offered to help us move our things. At that point, I was willing to do whatever it took just to see my baby. I needed to get a good look at him and **SEE** for myself that he was okay. Our conversation was cordial; much like friends. I didn't ask him many questions, allowing him to share with me whatever he wanted me to know. In return, I spoke to him with love in my voice, just as God had instructed me to do.

During the 2016 Spring Break, we made a somewhat unplanned trip to Atlanta because my grandmother had been extremely ill the previous two months and was finally leaving rehab to go home. Before rehab, she had spent a few weeks on life support. She and I were as thick as thieves, and to see her laid up would have devastated me. With her on the way home, I was ready to see her. My grandmother could no longer care for herself and moved in with my mom (I'm sure she would have rather been living with me. Not long before she went into the hospital, she decided to visit me and check out Houston but was never able to make the trip).

I had vowed I would never step foot in my mother's house again, yet I found myself breaking that vow to see my grandmother. Much to my surprise, my son was living with my parents! At first, I thought, *"Oh, he must have gone to Atlanta after turning 18 years old."* That didn't surprise me, as relocating to

Houston was a challenging transition for all of us, especially considering my children didn't want to leave Atlanta. But guess what? I later learned my son had been living with my parents **THE WHOLE TIME!**

NOT ONE PERSON WHO KNEW TOLD MY HUSBAND OR ME!!!

For two years, I cried, hurt, prayed, and pushed my way through each day. My parents, oldest daughter, two sisters, and some other relatives *KNEW* where my son was and not **ONCE** did they think to tell **ME—HIS MOTHER!** Have you any idea what it's like to not know where your child is? To not know if they are dead or alive? If they have eaten? If they are sick? If they are hurt? If they are being mistreated? Those questions and more ran through my mind daily *FOR TWO YEARS!* To know my own "family"—including my oldest daughter—would go to that length to hurt and betray me was astonishing!

I began to reflect on every phone call I had with my daughter after my son ran away, and she **NEVER** eluded to the fact that he was living in the same house with her! I've never been more hurt or felt more pain a day in my life. So many thoughts and memories of the various interactions with my family ran through my mind. I even recall hanging out at "Chacho's" restaurant one night with two of my cousins and them stating they "heard" my son was in Atlanta. They never explicitly said they knew for a fact; they just threw out the information like there was a lingering question waiting to be answered by me. If, after all, they knew for *SURE*, they would've told me outright, correct? I just blew it off like it was gossip or hearsay.

I found myself wondering what kind of people **KNOW** where their family member's child is, yet doesn't tell them? They knew I was in torment! I concluded my relatives must have had some serious hatred toward me. At that time, I felt I would have rather given natural childbirth 17 times back-to-back with **NO** meds, as opposed to enduring the pain I felt—a pain that eventually festered into hatred toward them.

Over time and with lots of prayer and coaching by God, He helped me to rid my heart of that bondage-like feeling. He renewed my spirit.

In March 2017, my mom called me from Atlanta airport, stating she and my dad were on their way to Houston. *Huh? What?* **[Blank stare.]** As you can imagine, that phone call caught me completely off-guard. By the grace of God alone, I was able to invite them into my home to spend time with us.

After they left, I was doing my walking laps around my neighborhood and talking with God, as I always did. *"You must forgive them,"* He said. I thought, *"Oh, geez; here He goes again!"* So, I asked Him, *"**WHY** do I have to forgive **THEM**? I didn't do **ANYTHING** to them, God!"* I know you're wondering what He said back, right? Haha!

Welp, in a stern voice, He replied, *"Because I require **MORE FROM YOU!** I EXPECT more from YOU!"*

I will never forget how His words rang through my body. I could tell He was serious and that I'd better get it together...**QUICKLY!**

To this day, not one person has taken responsibility nor apologized for their part in the situation. At this point, however, I could not care less. I'm doing very well with not having the apologies I'm sure I'll never receive. LOL!

God gave me an opportunity to find out what **TRUE** forgiveness was and how it was able to set **ME** free. I will never allow myself to be bound by the actions of others. Now, I'm not saying I don't feel emotions. What I **am** saying is that it isn't necessary to remain shackled to them for a lifetime. It's a waste of time and energy to hold on to a grudge. Doing so wouldn't have allowed me to grow and be who God created me to be! Being able to release all that hurt and pain made room for God to fill me up with unconditional love, compassion, empathy, and care for not only them but also for others. It also made room for Him to bless me more abundantly. God reminded me of how many times He had forgiven me, while still loving me as if I were flawless and perfect.

I have found that love is the cure. I pray I'm able to help many to see that. And, as my best friend Jay told me, *"That was a small situation to a giant, and you're a giant, Kish!"*

Compiled by Angela R. Edwards

Laurie Benoit

Dedication:
To all those who struggle every day with loving yourself…
Know that you are not alone. You are brave, you are capable, you are lovable, and you are uniquely, imperfectly YOU.

Bio:
Laurie Benoit is a wife and mother of four, residing in the village of Climax, Saskatchewan in Canada. Since 2014, she has become an International Best-Selling Author as a contributor in *"God Says I am Battle-Scar Free: Testimonies of Abuse Survivors – Parts 4 & 5"*, along with her own book, *"The Transformative Power of 'The Word'"*, which was released in 2019. She is also a Freelance Writer and Blogger. It has been her goal to bring awareness, offer hope, and to inspire change for others through her writing.

"A Not-So-Simple Love Story"

*"And then one day, she just began to breathe...
and for the first time ever, fell in love with life."*
© 2019 Author Laurie Benoit @ Once Awakened
www.facebook.com/onceawakened

Love. (noun) An intense feeling of deep affection or a great interest and pleasure in something. (Merriam-Webster, n.d.)

Life. (noun) The existence of an individual human being or animal. (Merriam-Webster, n.d.)

Is it really all that easy to love? Honestly, I wouldn't be able to tell you. *Love* has never come easy in my life, **no matter** who the relationship has been with — yet we all continue to do so, in the best manners we know.

I want to give you something to ponder for yourself: Do you **REALLY** love your life and the people who play such intricate roles in your daily happenings?

My answer is this: I do *NOW*, though I must admit it's been a very difficult lesson for me to learn just what it means to love others, myself, and life...and to **accept** that love. If there is one thing I have learned, it is this: Love is not conditional. You do not need permission from anyone to love yourself. You are the only one who knows what you need to make yourself happy.

However, it has been my experience that as a child grows through life, how we are raised affects how we grow to love others, ourselves, and life itself. We look up to the **adults** in our lives and often mimic their behaviors. We look to them for guidance, advice, and support, while silently watching them and picking up on their every little cue.

The question remains: **How does one learn how to love if they've never been shown or guided along the way?** In my personal experience, that journey is fraught with many trials and errors. We are all imperfect beings, learning our own lessons in the ways in which we were taught—whether directly or indirectly.

As for me, I spent an entire lifetime of not only **NOT** feeling love, but also not knowing how to love. Those few times when I did begin to feel like someone was starting to love and care for me, I didn't know how to react or reciprocate it, so I would self-destruct the situation. Years of abuse had conditioned me into believing I was unworthy of being loved. The hurtful actions and words of others replayed in my mind like a broken record, skipping over and over and over again. I truly hated myself and my life. In the deepest pits of my heart and soul, I began to honestly believe all the negative actions shown and comments said to me throughout the years.

Because of those deep-rooted thoughts, I also carried within me a deep, endless darkness. Many would call it "depression." Along with that silent partner came my strong belief of unworthiness of life itself. So, when I gained the courage to act upon my deepest, darkest thoughts, feelings, and beliefs, I tried to end my life. The two bottles of pills I had ingested most likely would have done the trick…had someone not found me.

Of course, it was at that time someone took notice and felt as though I might have needed help. I did, but honestly, by that time in my life, I was done asking for help. I had asked for help for many years—in fact, I pleaded for help, only to have the same outcome time and again: me not being listened to.

As a result of my failed attempt, I was locked away in a facility that was meant to "help," but I no longer cared for the support they wished to offer me. I shut down and refused to talk anymore.

Why was it that people only ***"seemed"*** to care about what I had to say when I tried to end my life? Did they really care, or was it just a façade? Who knows? Perhaps it was only out of concern of how "they" might look if a child in the system were to die a few years after being in their custody.

I was only 14 years old, yet I felt as though I had lived 114 years! I felt old and tired for my young, tender age.

I was frustrated and angry about not being heard. I was blamed and, worse yet, told that I deserved to be treated as I had always been. Of course, I didn't want help under those circumstances, coupled with the beliefs that were deeply ingrained in my thoughts!

So, as my life continued, I found myself in unhealthy and even dangerous situations and relationships. I relied on substances to numb my pains. I was angry about the vicious cycle that became my life. My daily journey became only about just coping…and surviving. It was not a pretty sight. In fact, I was truly messed up and miserable. I had so much baggage I had been carrying for so many years with no way to release it all. Each time I found an outlet for my feelings, it was used against me in the most horrific ways, leaving me feeling unable to trust others as well.

I lived a life of abuse that never seemed to have any end in sight. Along with that, the weight of my darkness covered me, leaving me always to wonder if life was actually worth the struggle and fight.

Also, in my experience, when one doesn't have anyone to look up to or mentor them, one often goes through life seemingly lost and stuck in unhealthy patterns and relationships—which, honestly, is just where I was.

Stuck.

Wanting.

Wishing.

Longing.

Unknowledgeable about how to love myself and life.

It seemed love was always just beyond my reach. If others saw me as unlovable and unworthy, I suppose there had to be some truth to it. The emotional and psychological damage I'd endured had many years to work its way through every recess of my mind. From childhood well into adulthood, I kept finding myself in the same type of relationships with different people. Each offered up new ways to help me self-destruct how I felt about myself and life. That applied to family and friends alike.

Eventually, at a real turning point in my life, my children were taken from me. Years of emotional and mental abuse had worn me down so much, and I wasn't even able to stand up and fight for them, let alone myself. Both my life and I were a real mess! I had one chance to change it and start moving forward.

At the time, I was well into my 20s (in fact, I wasn't very far from my 30s) when I was very fortunate to have a strong woman injected into my life. She was someone I could confide in, look up to, and help me to see that it was **only I** who could change the trajectory of my life. She helped me to see that it was **only I** who my children could rely on for safety and look up to. It was **only I** who would teach my children how they, too, would allow others to treat them in life.

Did I want my children to endure all that I had already gone through? ***HELL NO!*** I only wanted and wished a better life for them every day since their births. There was one problem, though: How could I achieve that and teach them, when I had been stuck in the vicious cycle myself?

Well, with a bit of help, the right support for me, and a personal commitment, I embarked on the most extensive task of my life: overhauling everything and everyone in my life. I began to release myself from those who held me down in the quicksand of negativity.

It started with one small change and moved forward from there. I let go of the substances that kept me numb to my pains. I found gainful employment. I started weaning out what was left of my social circle and kept only a few select friends. I moved and kept changing different aspects of my life as needed. As I began to tear myself free from the darkness that had become "my life," great strides were made towards a healthier brand of living.

When I finally began to feel the heaviness I carried for so many years ease up a little, I went on the search for an outlet to release all the baggage. I began writing—something that, for me, was a lifelong dream. At first, I penned poetry. Then, I began to give voice to my autobiography through writing, but alas, I was far from ready to release it all. I also became inundated with large doses of doubt when a family member "reminded" me about my lack of education and stated I could never achieve my goal of becoming a writer because of it (that was not the first time it was said to me throughout the course of my life, but it was definitely the most disheartening). I guess, truthfully, I should be grateful because, at the time, the signs of severe PTSD (Post-Traumatic Stress Disorder) pierced my mind like someone had just hit replay on every horror movie ever made. Nightmares upon nightmares filled my nights, waking me with horrible recollections that were not just nightmares; they were horrifying events that actually happened to me.

No wonder Dissociative Amnesia was present in my life. I wouldn't have wanted to remember…

So, I stopped writing for quite a long time to allow my mind time to calm the horrifying thoughts and memories. I picked the pen back up and began to write again years later.

I knew the time had arrived to begin writing again when I discovered and began to apply The Law of Attraction. I had come to take part in meditation, and in doing so, one day, I concentrated with the intent of finding the answer to the question: **What was I to do with my life?**

The answer came through loud and clear: Write and share your life story! Take time to also share some of life's small beauties with photography!

Life isn't all about one or the other. It's about balance, and to have beauty, we must also have chaos.

Well, my life since that time has been about just that: balance, beauty, chaos, love, and being genuine. I have never been perfect. I've made more than my fair share of mistakes and hurt people more often than I care to say; however, I am trying to become a better me, and that means accepting myself even for those things.

And so, it began…one topic at a time. I wrote about things that mattered to me, things I believed I could help change, and things I wished to change. I desired to provide hope for others, inspire them, and help them to heal. In the midst, I sought to find what I had been missing my whole life: love for myself, my life, and for each person I came across.

What could be better than that?

I must admit: It has taken me most of my life to realize I am worthy, capable, and deserve to be loved. It has taken a lot of tears, healing, and self-work to get to a point where I can finally take a deep breath in and just breathe, realizing I am the one in control of my own destiny.

Loving yourself, life, and even others is not a simple task for everyone. Some of us have to work diligently on those things. To those of you who have to work on building or rebuilding yourself and your life, know that you are worthy, you are loved, and you are lovable. Know that you have all the courage and strength needed to combat anything before you. Know that if I can transform my life, you certainly can, too!

I'm sending you love, strength, courage, and perhaps a bit more knowledge to help you along your journey.

Namaste. *"I bow to the divine in you."*

Marlowe R. Scott

Dedication:

Praises to my Savior, Jesus Christ, for constant **LOVE** and blessings too numerous to mention. To my daughter, Angela Edwards, whose **LOVE** and **SUPPORT** of my literary efforts are *AWESOME*!

Bio:

Marlowe Scott's God-given talents include authoring eight Best-Selling inspirational books, composing poetry, sewing, and crocheting. She shares God's **LOVE** on Facebook through her "Encouraging and Nourishing Words" group. Her prayer is that others be inspired to accept Jesus Christ as their personal Savior and grow in their Christian walk.

Compiled by Angela R. Edwards

"No Greater Love"

The word "LOVE" truly can be said to "cover a multitude of sins," as the familiar saying goes! That is stated clearly in the scriptures, where love is often referred to as "charity."

"And above all things, have fervent charity among yourselves: for charity shall cover the multitude of sins."
(1 Peter 4:8, KJV)

It is comforting to me knowing that God loves me and forgives His chosen people multiple times. To top it off, Jesus Christ came, taught, and sacrificed His Divine Life for those who confess their sins, repent, and believe He is the key to a promised Heavenly reward.

The Attributes of God

When growing and experiencing the **LOVE** of God, we discover so many ways we become sure He loves us. The following list shares a few:

- Loving
- Forgiving
- Merciful
- Faithful
- Righteous
- Powerful
- Mighty
- Sovereign
- Just

- Compassionate
- Gracious
- Good
- Holy
- Refuge
- Helper

Many examples of love are found in 1 Corinthians 13, which is often referred to as "The Love Chapter."

God loves mankind so much that **EVERY** aspect of our life is covered through the **TRINITY** — three persons in one:

- God is the Father and Creator.
- Jesus Christ is the Savior
- The Holy Spirit is the Comforter

The Trinity may not be understood and embraced by all; however, I pray that in time, clarification will be revealed to you.

Other examples are the Hebrew words that show God's **LOVE**. The three which follow are just a few:

1. YHWH - Yirah or Jireh, which is interpreted as YAHWEH: God will provide. A scriptural example can be found in Genesis 22:13-14, when Abraham was told to sacrifice his son, Isaac, and God provided a ram in the bush as the sacrifice instead.
2. YHWH - Rapha, meaning God that heals, as found in Exodus 15:26. This was when God made the bitter water of Marah sweet, and the people were able to be restored to health.

3. YHWH – Ra-ah is indicative of the Lord is my Shepherd, as found in Psalm 23:11. God guides and leads like a shepherd through joyful times, as well as difficult times in life.

Personal Experiences and God's Love Demonstrated to Me

In June 2019, I was inspired to compose and post a devotional titled "Encouraging and Nourishing Words" on Facebook. The theme verse is Romans 8:28 – *"And we know that all things work together for good to them that love God, to them who are the called unto His purpose"* (KJV). This verse has been proven time and again in my life.

Further inspiration comes from John 16:33 – *"These things I have spoken unto you, that in me, ye might have peace. In the world, ye shall have tribulation: but be of good cheer; I have overcome the world"* (KJV). Those words are comforting for sure!

An example of God's **LOVE** demonstrated in my life is the following short, personal experience. There have certainly been times in my 70+ years when I have needed "charity" from the world's point of view. While I have never been in the welfare system fully, I had applied for food stamps when my children were young. My amount allowed was not that much because I was employed.

Thinking back on those times, somehow, bills were paid, and food was available. When comparing the world's charity to what God gives, there's really **NO** comparison! God's charity *(LOVE)* is readily and constantly available without paperwork and stressing out, no matter what my circumstances may be. The charity received and promised by God had benefits and peace beyond measure. My cup runneth over many times! (A Psalm 23:5 reference.)

Another prime example from years ago was when I had to leave a new position on the job because of the pending birth of my son. Because I was there less than a year, I did not qualify for maternity leave benefits. My God — the Lover of my soul — again provided me weeks of provisions and made a way not only to return to the organization, but the reinstatement was done expediently! **WON'T GOD DO IT?!**

There are similar testimonies in my inspired books that document and assure me, as well as **GOD'S SAVED CHILDREN,** of His never-ending *LOVE* and provisions.

Just as everyone has, I have fallen short because of my actions and choices made through the years. Some were while I was young and naïve. For example, when I was dating, I thought relationships were like the romance magazines I read. **WRONG!** Talk about a wake-up call! I experienced lies, cheating, selfishness, and two of my suitors even considered me a "trophy" to display to others because of my shapely figure and long hair! I am sure others have experienced the same.

I am so blessed that **MY GOD** loves me just as I am! Today, I am older, overweight, bent over, slow-moving, and achy! Just think about it: Would those same men have stuck around with me and shown me off now?

THE POINT HERE IS THIS: GOD LOOKS AT THE INSIDE OF OUR HEART AND SOUL. Conversely, *humanity* looks at and judges based on the outer appearance.

Following are a few more relevant scriptures to read and be blessed by:

- Psalms 116:1-2
- Romans 8:28, 35, 37
- 1 Corinthians 2:9
- Hebrews 13:8
- 1 Peter 4:8
- 1 John 4:16

One of the spiritual gifts God provides to comfort and encourage us while showing His **LOVE** are the hymns written over the ages. In closing, I will share three verses of a hymn written in 1719 by Isaac Watts entitled *"God, Our Help in Ages Past"*:

Verse 1: Our God, our help in ages past, our hope for years to come, our shelter from the stormy blast and our eternal home.

Verse 3: Before the hills in order stood, or Earth received her frame, from everlasting, you are God, to endless years the same.

Verse 7: Our God, our help in ages past, our hope for years to come; O be our guard while troubles last, and our eternal home.

In concluding this brief sharing, I believe this information may help you. I am a woman who loves to search out interesting biblical facts. In the King James Version of the Holy Bible, there are 310 occurrences of the word "love." The Old Testament has 131 of them, with the remaining 179 in the New Testament. I do not know for sure, but because there are more in the New Testament, it makes me think that with the birth of Jesus Christ, His ministries, and the works and testimonies of the disciples and Christian converts, demonstrated **LOVE** becomes more evident.

Prayerfully, you have been enlightened, strengthened, and encouraged by knowing there is truly *NO GREATER LOVE* than that which is found in God! May those who have not accepted salvation through Jesus Christ be receptive to the LOVE, peace, and protection lovingly being extended to you.

JESUS LOVES YOU, THIS I KNOW!

FOR THE BIBLE TELLS ME SO!

I have been blessed to author seven inspirational books. One has been published as a trilogy of the first three, and the last is a children's book encouraging children to learn their ancestry. The titles are:

- *Spiritual Growth: From Milk to Strong Meat*
- *Believing Without Seeing: The Power of Faith*
- *Keeping It Real: The Straight and Narrow*
- *Worth the Journey: The Train Ride to Glory (trilogy)*
- *"I AM" Cares: His Eyes Are on the Sparrow*
- *Never Alone: Intimate Times with Jesus*
- *Plentiful Harvest: Fertile Ground*
- *Talli's Ancestry Surprise: Beginning the Ancestral Search*

The books are available on Amazon or through the publisher's website at www.PearlyGatesPublishing.com.

Compiled by Angela R. Edwards

Natosha Lovall

Dedication:

I would like first to thank God because, without Him, none of this would be possible. To Mrs. Angela Edwards: Thank you for giving me an opportunity to tell my story.

Bio:

Natosha Lovall is a now 2-time author, with all thanks given to Mrs. Angela Edwards and Tosha Dearbone. She is the Founder of "The Lov-All Foundation," a nonprofit organization with a mission to create a world where **EVERYONE** matters. Their motto is to put #LoveInAction. Natosha is also a Mentor and the Vice-President of "Positive Express," an all-girl mentoring organization with a focus on building self-esteem. She also volunteers and helps those less fortunate than others. Natosha states, *"I love being a blessing because I am most definitely* **BLESSED***!"*

"To Love and Be Loved...God's Way"

I didn't think **LOVE** would ever find me again after all I'd been through. For a long time, I told myself I wouldn't give my heart to anyone else. That quickly changed when "JDH" walked into my life.

I remember it like it was yesterday. When I first laid eyes on him, we made an instant connection. He was working at the time (we worked in the same facility) and, when I walked in, he smiled at me with his baby face that displayed his beautiful dimples. My heart just melted! It was as if I just knew he was "the one."

As I was getting on the elevator, a coworker/friend of mine was getting on as well. Just as she was about to enter, JDH ran over to speak to her and hugged her. I knew she was not someone he was seeing because she was much older than him, so, of course, I asked her, *"Who was that?"* I failed to hide my excitement.

"He's a relative of mine," she replied.

"YES! YES! YES!" was all that flowed through my head at that moment.

I asked a little bit more about him and told her how I found him so adorable. She then invited me to one of their family gatherings that she said he would for sure be attending. I happily agreed to go. I was really excited about meeting him, so I made sure I was looking cute when I arrived.

My coworker introduced the two of us, and we hit it off very well. From that first meeting, we continued communicating, which led to a relationship. Now, just as I stated, I wasn't ready for a relationship and didn't expect love to find me, but it happened nonetheless.

JDH was so different from all the other men in my past. He showed me how a woman was really supposed to be treated. He wasn't at all selfish, loved me for me, and was a provider and giver. He loved doing and buying things for me. He had me spoiled rotten, which was something I wasn't used to. I was, after all, always the one on the giving end in my previous relationships.

We started spending a lot of time together, and he fell for me first. I could tell he was a little afraid because he had fallen in love with me so fast. We ended up moving in together, and everything was great at first. We did virtually everything together. He wasn't used to a person like me because he was my polar opposite; he was the type to live life "inside a box" and hadn't experienced life as I did. We took vacations together and did other things he had never done. All the while, our love deepened more and more. He was so affectionate and attentive—things I loved about him. He wasn't afraid to express his love for me all day, every day. His family even noticed a significant change in him once I became a part of his life. He had let his guard down and was receiving the love he had always wanted…and so was I.

Another thing I loved about him was that he never wanted to see me stressed out about anything. I remember the days when I would come home from work, and before my children could bombard me with requests to do things for them, he would make sure I relaxed first before doing anything. He would tell the children, *"Let your mom rest a little from working a hard day. Whatever it is you need, I got you. Just come to me."* Whatever they needed, he made sure they had it!

Everything was going great for quite some time between JDH and me, but then, he started pulling away because he was scared he would get hurt. He fought himself behind his own insecurities. I didn't know then but later learned he had abandonment issues from childhood that were the root cause of his fear. Soon, things started to change between us. He and his routine changed as well. He started hanging out later than usual. Sometimes, he didn't even come home at a decent hour — and didn't see anything wrong with it! I accepted it the first time it happened because I'm sure I believed whatever lie it was that he told me. When it continued to happen, I refused to allow myself to put up with his mess. He wanted to keep up with his peers and entertain multiple women. He also started drinking, which made it and his attitude worse. He would get upset about the tiniest thing and ignore me as if I wasn't standing directly in front of him. It would be like he was looking through a glass window.

I could tell the loved we once had was fading. At the same time, I wanted him to love me the way he used to. I didn't want to believe he was cheating on me because I thought he loved me, but in my heart, I knew he was. I never went looking for proof, but God always showed me. JDH got really sloppy with his actions, eventually proving my suspicions were correct.

Now, because I had been through being cheated on before, I didn't react the way he expected. I looked at things as his loss and just wanted to know the reason why. Often, we would be in the same household and not say one word to each other for weeks at a time. One thing I do respect him for is that he would never allow the children to see us upset with one another, and he never treated them differently despite our situation. It got to the point where I could no longer put up with his shenanigans, so one day, while he was at work and the children were at school, I packed up our things and moved out.

Even though I packed up and moved out, I was still very much in love with him and wanted to be with him, but my feelings were deeply hurt. I ended up staying with a friend for about a month before moving into my own place.

I fell into a deep depression because I could not bring myself to get over him. Although I knew he wasn't faithful, I still saw some good in him. Plus, he was a great manipulator. After being apart for a while and giving myself time to get over him (at least that's what I thought was happening), we started communicating again "as friends." We actually became the best of friends and talked to each other about any and everything we had going on in life. He apologized for everything he had done and put me through, and I felt his apology was sincere. He even apologized to the children.

We agreed to hang out as "just friends," but eventually, it became more than that. We started being intimate, causing the feelings we once shared to blossom again. I believed I could handle it because we were "just friends" with no strings attached. If either of us spent time with anyone else on the side, we agreed to be upfront with each other about it. Well, I kept my part of the bargain, but, of course, he did not. At that point, with us being as close as we were, there shouldn't have been anything he lied to me about.

He stopped answering the phone after a certain time, and I couldn't just pop up at his place anytime I wanted to anymore. I found out he had a girlfriend and didn't want to tell me! He would lie and say she was not his girlfriend, though. I believed him after a while because others lied for him as well. He was just **THAT** good at manipulating a situation!

I continued to deal with him for almost a year until one day, I got on social media and the person he was supposedly not in a relationship with made a post about being married to her wonderful husband for ten months! **THAT** was a shocker to me because I don't deal with married men nor men in relationships. Not knowing if her post was real (that woman was hell on wheels and a bit out of her mind), I needed proof of my own. I logged onto the Harris County Clerk's website and saw all I needed to see. Proof positive! JDH and her were, indeed, married!

I was furious, hurt, and disappointed. **How could he put me in such a horrible position?** I then brought my newfound information to his attention and let him know I was **DONE** with him. I told him, *"You will reap what you sow. You are going to meet your match one day!"*

Boy, was I right!

JDH's wife gave him so much hell, and he fell into a deep depression. After only a few months of being married, he had lost so much. I could have been the one to say, ***"You deserved it!"*** because he did, but I'm not the one he had to answer to. **GOD** showed him he needed to humble himself and treat others the way he wanted to be treated.

He again apologized to me for his actions and felt like he deserved what he received because of how he treated me. I am a woman of God, and **GOD** would not allow me to throw something like that in JDH's face. Instead, God humbled me. I was there to help him get through his depression, with the difference being, I was truly "just a friend." He needed someone, and God obviously put me in his life for a reason.

By then, I knew my worth. I found me again and was strong enough to do what God put me in his life to do: help him heal. I wouldn't allow myself to hurt him just because he had hurt me. He needed to grow and love himself first in order to give that same love back.

He put his pride to the side, built a better relationship with his mom, and became a totally different person. He became the man I saw in him when we first met. He started studying the scriptures I shared with him and really started believing God could heal him, just as He had healed me. I was so happy and proud of JDH when he finally found God. He was then able to heal, find himself, and be happy again with life.

At that moment, I knew God put us on each other's paths for a reason. He brought JDH into my life to show me what real **LOVE** was and how a woman should be treated. He also showed me what a woman should not put up with. I believe I was put into his life to teach him how to humble himself and set his pride aside.

We both learned lessons throughout it all, but most of all, we learned how to **LOVE** and be **LOVED**…the way *GOD* wanted us to.

Reyna Harris-Goynes

Dedication:
I dedicate my story to my husband and children, who have been an inspiration to and showed me what love truly means today.

Bio:
Reyna Harris-Goynes is a mother of five, as well as a wife to an amazing husband whom she's known since middle school. Her family is the joy of her life, and she cherishes them more than they can imagine. She has endured many trials in life, but becoming an author has truly made a difference in how she can lay claim to being victorious today. She volunteers for an organization called "Positive Express," and has known the Founder, Tosha Dearbone, for quite a while. Reyna excitedly states, *"I look forward to what is in store for my life and my family!"*

Compiled by Angela R. Edwards

"With Pain Comes Strength and Love"

In my lifetime, I have loved, been loved, and am loved; however, I wasn't receiving the love I wanted at one point in my life. I desired the type of love a daughter first has with her father, so I began searching for love in the wrong places. That search led me to look for it from boys who didn't know what "love" meant or how even to love themselves.

SIDEBAR: Choosing to look for love through boys/men is the wrong thing to do for any girl or woman. Look to God — the source of *TRUE* love.

Growing up, some children have the fortune of being raised with both parents in the home. Some have one. In my case, I had none…even though I lived in the same house as my mom.

I then started having children, and that's where my true love came from — in more ways than one. My children were everything to me, even though they had people talking negatively about me to them. I have never put a man before my children because I knew when that man was gone, my children would always be there. The love I had for my children was indescribable, and I felt that same level of care from them as well. I then entered a relationship I knew should have never been.

SIDEBAR: When you try to give a person the benefit of the doubt, it might be at the wrong time because they don't feel the same way as you do.

As my relationship with God grew, I started to see and know that love wasn't supposed to hurt, especially not by a person who claimed to love me dearly.

SIDEBAR: When a person truly loves you, they do everything in their power to keep you happy by any means necessary. You shouldn't have to go through trauma to feel loved and appreciated by someone who's supposed to care for you.

Leaning on God will have you loving on yourself more and more because you must first love yourself before any others, including your family. As for me, I have never really felt the love from my family because I always felt as if I was the proverbial "Black Sheep" of the family. I was always treated differently. Although it hurt, I actually got used to it. I don't know if it was because I was always the rebellious one who didn't want to be told what to do, but the difference in treatment was evident. Without God on my side keeping me close, I don't know where I would be, especially with not feeling the love I yearned for and needed.

Over the years, I have been in and out of relationships/friendships that were toxic and failed to provide the love I wanted and needed in my life. I tried hard to make things work with each relationship I encountered, including those with family members. I know now that removing myself from certain situations was very healthy for me because it kept down the confusion and out of the way of others' nonsense. Some of the relationships weren't good for me, so they most definitely weren't suitable for my children either. I supposed it helped to the degree that I never placed a large amount of trust in any one person, which made it easy for me to walk away from them.

The relationship I'm in now is one I've waited for years to happen. I'm enjoying every moment of it daily. Before coming together, we lived different lifestyles, which proved to separate us in our younger years. Now, we're living life one day at a time. We've had our fair share of bumps and bruises over the years, but God didn't reunite us for us to be apart. The love we have for each other has grown so strong, we have become one. I have so much respect and love for my husband because he loves me for who I am. He's everything I've ever wanted in someone: Love me and all my flaws, no matter what.

Although we rarely get any alone time or go out on date nights, we are still going strong—much to the disappointment of those folks who were counting on us to fail. I have always had strong feelings for my husband, but I knew he didn't really want to be in a relationship "back then," so we spoke a lot on the phone at first. At the age of 16, my now-husband went to prison. For the longest time, I never knew why he told me to move on with my life. While "away," he stopped responding to my letters. When I had the opportunity to ask why, he stated it was because my mom told him to leave me alone because she didn't approve of his lifestyle at the time. Well, everyone makes mistakes, and he has since learned from them. People deserve a second chance, no matter what they did in life.

I know I can't live without him and the love he has for me. It's not because I need or want something from him...besides his *love*. We have been through so much over the last few years, but we're still standing together and staying strong. So many times, we thought about giving up, but God said otherwise and kept us together (and sane). When our daughter was born, that brought us closer together and made the love we shared even stronger. Regardless of what others said or thought about us, we pressed forward and moved on with our lives…together.

My husband is one of the most caring, kind, nurturing, protective, and awesome people I know. It has been an amazing journey in life to be with someone of that nature. I never knew how love felt until I met my husband, and it's an indescribable feeling. Even though some days are better than others, I am at a happy place in life, and my husband does his part to ensure I remain that way. When I sit back and think about my life without him, I'm sure it would be miserable and spiraling out of control to the extent that no one (but God) knows.

For the longest time, I thought I would never be loved, feel loved, or know what love really feels like in any way or from anyone, including my family. When I decided I wanted better and different for my life, I knew deep down in my heart that my husband was the right one to make that happen. In response, I went after what I wanted and found him. I hadn't even thought about "love" because he had long ago given up on it himself. I gave up on love, too, but I heard God say, "I have you covered, Reyna." I refused to give up because I did what God and my heart instructed me to do. This day, it has been the best decision I've made in a very long time.

Before I started looking for my husband, I was very miserable and depressed. Today, I am happy and very cheerful! I have since learned my happiness is everything, and I give my husband credit where credit is due. Together, we have come so far in this thing we call "Life and Love." The ride has been interesting (to say the least), but we aren't giving in or giving up!

SIDEBAR: When you are tossed and driven by a few storms in life, you must keep fighting — and fight to win! Don't let the devil get the victory!

My son has been sick for almost two years. Both my husband and I had a feeling it was going to be the deal-breaker for us. We were wrong! We have been shown who's there for us…and who's not. Our support system during this difficult time in minimal at best, family included. The journey hasn't been easy for either of us, but we still show each other so much support, which is how we're able to keep going hard for my son. It's as if everyone turned their backs on us since my son fell ill. Throughout it all, my husband and I have held it together, even when we were stressed out.

SIDEBAR: When you have so much love and concern for another, loving them comes easy. Whatever may be hindering their journey can be quickly addressed because your only concern is making them happy. There's nothing quite like knowing you are truly loved and cared for, so be grateful for everything God has done for you.

I genuinely love and cherish everything about my husband. He's the type of man who goes above and beyond for everyone except himself. (I'm still working on getting him to put himself first — a lesson I'm learning at the same time.) God has told me I still have some work to do, and although the struggle is real at times, my husband and I got this! Learning to love yourself and your spouse at the same time is a challenge all in itself, but we are up for the challenge.

SIDEBAR: When it's all said and done, you're the one who needs to love you the most. Anything that comes after that is a bonus!

Sometimes, taking a break from life rejuvenates you. Spend time loving yourself even more because you'll need that energy to one day relax and begin again. Taking life one day at a time really helps with learning how to love me more every day. Why? Because when others turn their backs on me, there's no stress! I don't have to concern myself with being upset because someone let me down when I needed them the most.

At one point, I had given up on loving myself as well as finding someone to love me for me, not for what I can and can't do for them. I know God puts people in our lives for a reason and definitely a season, but I had to figure out who was real and who wasn't. When jealousy is present, love cannot dwell within a relationship, so I had to be on the lookout for the ones who were trying to use me instead of loving me. I had to sit back, weigh my options, and weed out those who didn't love me like they claimed they did.

I have come so far since I started to love and really care for myself more than others. I used to worry about what others thought about me. Did they genuinely care? Eventually, it became clear that they didn't. When I stopped caring about what others thought about me, I started living my life as I should have from the beginning. I should've only cared about what God gave me: **LIFE!** Without Him, I don't know where I would be today.

I know more than anything that I'm in a happy place. I love myself and am loved by an awesome, loving person sent by God. We were reunited in God's perfect timing, not just because that's what I wanted. I give all praises to God for His help and guidance as He led me to my husband.

I AM AT PEACE! I AM LOVED!

Shanericka Jones

Dedication:

I dedicate this story to God — the head of my life — and to those who also feel hopeless. Life is possible. Stay Encouraged!

Bio:

Shanericka Jones is a published author and the Founder of "Prayer Works of Houston," a 501(c)(3) nonprofit. Her first solo literary venture is titled *Healing Through Hurts Prayer Journal*, and she is presently working on her second project. She remains active in the community by encouraging young women and men through difficult times and continues to partner with organizations with similar missions. Heading towards greatness, Shanericka is continually looking for ways to ignite life into those who feel hopeless, helpless, and depressed.

Compiled by Angela R. Edwards

"Just Call Me 'Self-Control'"

Through the years, life hasn't been all that bad...but it hasn't been all that good, either. I was born into a somewhat sheltered environment due to my mom having me at the age of 17, which prompted many of our conversations to include her repeating, *"I know I don't need any more babies."* That was the statement I allowed to create a wedge between my mom and me. My ears closed to everything she had to say.

I am so grateful God didn't close my heart because He, of course, already knew all that my life would entail. He also knew everything that my mom taught me, I would eventually go back and pick up that knowledge to help me through the rest of my life, even to this present day.

I have several memories that stand out, starting from the age of three until the age of 12. I recall being molested by several family members on both sides of the family. Those interactions sent me into a very lonely place. When those "situations" occurred, I was told not to say anything and that no one would believe me. At an early age, those lies taught me how to hide and not speak up when I was violated. The snatching of my innocence numbed me in so many ways. If I knew then what I know now, I would have told everyone who would have listened. I would have told someone about what was going on with me so that I could get help and live a life free of the abuse.

The next major event that shook my world in a massive way was the death of my maternal grandmother, who died in a house fire in 1988. When she passed, I felt as if my best friend had been taken from me. I no longer had someone to take me for rides on Sundays or bring me breakfast when she came in from work. For me, her death was the icing on the cake.

I started searching for comfort, a way of escape, love, friendship, and security. Instead of finding those things in a positive way, I indulged in self-destructive behaviors that included using mind-altering substances and promiscuous activities. During my search, nothing else significant happened; however, my past was enough to cause me to form some horrible habits that would seem to be unshakeable.

My mom worked a good majority of the time because she had to, so I spent a lot of time at someone else's house where she thought I was safe. My dad was a present-absent father, meaning he was there but did not fill the role of a father. He was more of a friend. That sort of unbalanced parenting allowed some horrible demons to grow inside of me. A life full of negative self-care flourished.

As I continued to grow in tolerance to escape my reality, I also noticed that the appetite for telling lies for no good reason started to become automatic during those times. I could have avoided so much pain if I had realized I could have opened my mouth and shared how sad and lonely I felt inside, how much I missed my grandmother, being molested, and not wanting to return to those people's houses anymore. Sadly, that wasn't a part of the plan for my life, so my choices created a lack of trust between the ones who loved me the most and me.

I had the pleasure of being married for a spell to the son of a king. That man treated me like a queen and set the standards high regarding how I should be treated by **all** men. After a year and a half of marriage, my husband died in a motorcycle accident in October 2003. The loss of my love caused my life to change in a way in which I lost it all for a brief moment. I became severely depressed, almost entirely dependent on substances, reckless in my actions, and suicidal.

In the span of 12 years, I managed to get myself into legal trouble three times, lost more than half my teeth, messed up my driving record, survived a couple of failed suicide attempts, gave birth to a daughter, and am currently a senior in college…for the last 14 years.

In March 2015, my mom handed me the deed to my lot at Paradise Cemetery. It was then I realized I was going to die as an addict if I didn't do something extremely different with my life. I searched for a rehabilitation facility, but couldn't find one in Texas. I then called a pastor who helped individuals get their lives together by sending them to rehabs across America. He told me there was a bed ready and waiting for me in Minnesota. I told him I would drive there. It took me two days to reach my destination on Currie Avenue.

When I arrived, I cried out to God, *"Lord Jesus, it's now or never! I need Your help!"* I felt more determined than ever. The program I entered was wonderful. It allowed me to meet some awesome people with whom I created some beautiful friendships along the way. The program incorporated a curriculum geared towards a Bible study that connected the Bible with tools that help in one's life. Much to my great disappointment, the program closed after one month of me being there due to lack of funding. Still, that one month I spent there was enough to plant a healthy seed of self-control. For the first time in my life, I had blossomed into a responsible woman.

I was over 1,500 miles away from home, so returning to my mom's house was not going to happen. I chose to depend on and worship God with everything in me. I needed His guidance and direction in my life.

Not too much longer after the rehab closed, I got pregnant. That pregnancy caught me by surprise but nevertheless, I was excited! I was going to gain a little prince whom God knew I would need in place because some more difficult moments were coming. I was able to find a job and stable housing, too. Being that my daughter was in Texas, I asked my mom if I could come home so that my children could grow up together. After discussing it with my stepdad, she said yes. Once I relocated back home, I gave birth to my son, found a stable job, and was determined to reclaim all I gave to the devil.

While on an extended stay in the Texas Department of Corrections, I had nothing but time to think and reflect. I told myself I should start a resource center called "Prayer Works" (the name at the time the vision came). It was during that time in 2011 that *"Prayer Works of Houston"* was birthed. The purpose of the organization is to help those needing resources in different areas of their lives.

Upon returning home, God has allowed me to do just that. The ministry, *"Prayer Works of Houston,"* has since been launched and hosts events throughout the year. We operate as an outreach ministry that helps, encourages, and provides resources that will allow individuals to ignite or reignite self-love, jumpstart their thought-processes, and help them find their niche or what makes them happy for the long haul so that they can be their best "self" in life. We offer workshops ranging from building a resume to rebuilding self-love.

On March 13, 2015, God began to reveal and unleash His Fruit of the Spirit within me and my life. Through faithfulness, I can walk in self-control and no longer live the way I want. Instead, I embrace the kindness and goodness God wills for me. I allow God's love through His Word to teach me self-love, which ultimately grants me peace and joy — things I wouldn't trade for the world, although it can be trying at times.

I have learned that life is great, and, with work and obedience, God has been wowing me daily. With God, I have been able to use self-control in all areas of my life that have allowed me to reach more than my full potential. I no longer limit myself, as I have learned to remember what God thinks of me when times are a little turbulent…such as when my mom died. If any moment would have been one to crack and throw in all the towels, I thought that would have been "it." God reminds me daily (in the gentlest of ways) that although I have survived some depressing, hopeless times, the BEST is yet to come!

Learning how to use my resources and relying on God's wisdom allows me to be a Published Author, Founder of an outreach ministry, Mentor, and a host of other great titles that I am blessed to carry. Rest assured of this one thing: As long as God blesses me with breath in my body, I will continue to serve Him however He sees fit. I trust that the result will be me and all those attached to me being continuously **BLESSED** beyond measure!

Tosha Dearbone

Dedication:
I dedicate this story to my children, my family, and any others who may have encountered rejection that caused them to waver with having a spiritual relationship with *"Love."*

Bio:
Tosha Dearbone was born in Urania, Louisiana and raised in Houston, Texas. She is a mother of four, grandmother of one, Community Advocate, Mental Health Aid, Founder of "Positive Express," Certified Medical Assistant, Certified Nursing Assistant, Certified Community Health Worker, Mentor of Harris County Juvenile, and an International Best-Selling Author. Tosha specializes in medical care, educating young ladies and women about HIV and AIDS, domestic/sexual violence, self-esteem, and is a voice for breaking generational curses. Tosha can be reached on social media at Tosha R. Dearbone and via email at trdearbo@yahoo.com.

"Love Wins!"

As I sit here penning my story, I find myself reminiscing about the void left in my heart from not hearing the words *"I love you."* My 'Love Story' dates back to the age of seven when I was left trying to understand why God took my daddy away from me at such a tender, young age.

You see, my daddy was very sick, although I never knew until my brother and I were picked up from school early one day. As we zoomed through traffic, it seemed as though my mother was in a rush to get to wherever we were heading. As she frantically made her way to our destination, I just sat and stared out of the window in wonder. When we finally arrived, I immediately noted we were at the hospital. We exited the car, rushed inside, and, upon entering the building, things went kind of fast from there.

I remember walking up to a room with the blinds closed and hearing the words, *"He is gone,"* echo throughout the room. I was numb and in disbelief. My daddy — out of **ALL** people — had *died*. I asked myself aloud, *"Why?"* I was a Daddy's Girl and hadn't spent enough time with him for him to be gone so soon. At that moment, I recall being told he had pneumonia and became very ill.

Days, months, and years seemed to fly by. My broken heart remained; beating, of course, but not with as much passion as before. I yearned for affection. I wanted to be loved, accepted, and valued. Growing up the only girl in a home with my mother and brothers, one would think I was spoiled rotten.

NOT! Instead of being told *"I love you"* and *"You are enough,"* I was cast down with words that included insults such as:

"Nobody's going to want you."

AND

"You're fat and out of shape."

In response to the verbal abuse, I found myself staying out of the way while trying to dodge the hurtful, wordy darts thrown at me. I often sat alone in my room, crying. I hid my truth behind a smile when others would see me. At the time, I felt the overall level of acceptance of me was **zilch**.

At the age of 15, I began "dating" this boy and heard (for the first time in a **LONG** time), *"I love you."* Those words melted my heart. I was all smiles and ready to do **anything** with and for him. As time passed by, I began to see that his *"I love you"* was fictional. His real intention was to have sex with me while he cheated and told other females he loved them, too. I was hurt and confused. **Why me?** He continued to play games with my heart for about another year, which sent me into a whirlwind of emotions.

In the two years he and I were together, I got pregnant…twice. The first time, I was told I had to get an abortion. The second time, I was asked, *"What do you want to do?"* I recall saying, *"I will keep it."* I believed that having a baby would give me some form of comfort from **someone** who would love me. In February 1997, I delivered my baby. A beautiful, brown-skinned girl who weighed in at 6 pounds, 3 ounces with a head full of curly hair, she was my everything.

I just **knew** her arrival would cause her father to change his ways, but I was wrong. Not even two months after her birth, he was caught cheating with someone I knew. Talk about hurt and disappointed! I then broke up with him and focused solely on my baby girl.

It wasn't long after our breakup before depression found its place in my life. *"No one loves me"* was my daily cry. It was as if I was no good to anyone if I wasn't giving them something. As such, it didn't take me long to fall for yet another person who treated me the same way. That time, though, he wasn't just cheating; he was abusing me and in and out jail. He once asked if his mother and siblings could live with me, and I said, *"Yes!"*

In hindsight, I believe I agreed to the arrangement because I felt that it would change him. Instead, it had me feeling like a big fool for allowing not just him to use me, but also his mother. The situation was critical.

- My car was taken when I was asleep.
- My jewelry came up missing.
- Let me not forget to mention she didn't help with rent, bills, or food.

All I could do was cry and ask, *"Why, Lord? Why do I continue to be hurt by people I thought loved me?"*

By that time, I had two children with no change in my circumstance. I was still "alone."

The pattern seemed to repeat itself through the years to follow. I would enter relationship after relationship, seeking the love I so desperately desired. I kept having children, feeling void after void with man after man. My mom and brothers were doing their own thing and living their best lives, while I just withered away in suicidal thoughts, emotional hurt, and isolation. In my quiet time, I thought, *"Life **can't** get any worse than this!"*

I remember the day I asked my mom, *"Why is it so easy for me to forgive the people who hurt me?"* Sadly, she didn't have an answer, causing me to further push my feelings to the side.

One day, my oldest daughter began to be rebellious against me, and I couldn't figure out why. She would tell me, **"I HATE YOU!"** They were harsh words; I know. It wasn't until 2015 when I finally outright asked her, *"Why do you say that to me?"*

She hunched her shoulders and said, *"I don't know."*

That answer wasn't good enough for me. I wanted to know her reasoning, so I pressed and continued to ask her, **"Why? Why? Why?"**

She finally gave in and said, *"Because you never show affection. You rarely tell my siblings and me that you love us."*

Now, that caught me off-guard. Immediately, I began having flashbacks on my own situations while growing up. I started to cry. I didn't know how to explain to my child that I was only doing the same thing to them by treating them the way I was when I was young. I was both hurt and disappointed in myself because I never wanted my children to experience a lack of love, even though they were growing up in a one-parent household. I didn't want to be the one they despised because they felt unloved and unwanted.

Instantly, I cried out to God to help me fix my ways and allow me to see beyond the actions of others who had broken my heart into a million tiny pieces in the past. I asked God to teach me how to love them, even if I didn't receive love in return.

As life would have it, in 2017, I was positioned back in a situation of having to live with my mom. When I tell you I prayed, I mean I prayed…and prayed…and prayed— **constantly**. My mom and I didn't see eye-to-eye on so many things, yet there I was in her environment without a real solution to living on my own again.

One day, I was asked to be a part of my first collaborative project, *Walk with Her: Wisdom for a Teenage Journey*. Little did I know: God was about to use that book as an opportunity for me to open up and be honest about the way I felt. I remember my mom reading my story…and crying. My daughter was the one to tell her I was only speaking my truth and that she couldn't be upset with me. My mother agreed with her, and that pathway to healing the relationship with my mom began. Shortly after, I felt my world come tumbling down once again when one of my brothers spoke death over me. When he tried to apologize, I said to him, *"You spoke how you really felt about me."* I then packed up my children and went to stay in a hotel. We stayed there for about a week before I said to myself, **"I cannot live like this!"** We had no choice but to return to my mother's house.

Even amid the hurt, all I could hear God say to me was, *"Forgive and let it go."* Thankfully, it became easier each day to adhere to God's instruction. Although it may sound crazy to some, I loved them all — even when they didn't love me (at least, that's what I thought).

Fast-forward to December 2018. I had an identity crisis where I found myself in a very dark place. Everyone around me was clueless. Once again, I began having suicidal thoughts, all while doing so much good and having a positive impact on the lives of others. After dealing with the hidden pain for so many years, I finally sought out help.

I went to work and told my manager that I needed to talk to someone. She said she understood and directed me to contact the Employee Help Department. I made an appointment and met with a woman who was the equivalent of a professional therapist. I recall her looking through my employee file and asking me questions about all that I do. I told her about my organization, being an author, my days in Houston, and more. She stopped me, looked me up on Google, and said, *"You do all of this, and you are thinking about doing **WHAT** again?"*

I was caught off-guard! I started stuttering and said, *"I know. It doesn't make sense."* After all, I thought I was over feeling unloved.

That woman began to speak life into me, making me realize that all of my greatness could not go to waste. She then suggested I see a professional therapist, and I did. It was my first time doing so in my 30+ years of life. Wow!

So, I went to see the therapist, and she said the same things to me! She also helped me to realize my triggers and that I wasn't suffering from depression, but rather an emotional disorder. Any time rejection reared its ugly head, that was where I found myself "stuck." I no longer wanted to feel that way, so I approached my pastor one Wednesday after Bible Study and told him all that was going on with me. We immediately went into prayer and, afterward, he asked, *"Do you feel anything?"*

I responded, *"Yes! I feel lighter and free!"*

With all that had occurred, I can now say with complete honesty that **I love me** and have found it much easier to love others, even when they have done me wrong. I've learned that me loving them doesn't take away the fact that my love outweighs any rejection or setback.

"For God so loved the world, that He gave His Only Begotten Son, that whomsoever believeth in Him shall not perish, but have everlasting life."

~ John 3:16, KJV ~

LOVE WINS!

Conclusion: God's Love is for ALL

As you may now see, "LOVE" means something different to virtually everyone. In *God's Love Fruit*, there is one commonality:

GOD'S LOVE REDEEMS!

Through each story penned in this book, it should be evident that God's love has been shown, despite one's circumstance, trial, or tribulation. Hence, we are given a **choice** to either pursue a personal relationship with Him or reject His love.

God is no fool. He knows we will fail. He knows we will break His heart. However, we can humbly approach His throne, repent, and ask for forgiveness.

In the Holy Bible, Mark tells of an instance when a man fell to his knees before Christ and begged, *"If You are willing, You can make me clean."* Filled with compassion, Christ responded, *"I am willing; be clean."* (See Mark 1:40-41.) Our gracious God allows for us to acknowledge His provision for our lives and be made whole.

We do not have to operate in a state of perpetual brokenness. The stories within this book have proven that! The authors have overcome abuse, rejection, abandonment, suicide, and so much more. Today, they are enveloped in God's LOVE and chose to use this platform to encourage and uplift YOU.

The question for you is this:

Considering what you've read and learned, will you receive God's LOVE today?

Tell God ALL about it!

What's **YOUR** "LOVE" Story? What have **YOU** overcome and desire to encourage others to do the same? Write it down and, if you are so led, share it with others. **BE FREE FROM THAT "THING" TODAY!**

_____

_____

_____

_____

_____

_____

_____

_____

_____

_____

_____

_____

_____

Compiled by Angela R. Edwards

God's Love Fruit

Compiled by Angela R. Edwards

About the Compiler

Angela R. Edwards is the CEO and Chief Editorial Director of Pearly Gates Publishing, LLC (PGP) and Redemption's Story Publishing, LLC (RSP) — Award-Winning International Christian Book Publishing Houses located in Houston, Texas. In May 2018, PGP was honored as the 2018 Winner of Distinction for Publishing in South Houston, Texas, by the Better Business Bureau (BBB). In 2019, she was awarded BBB Gold Star Certificates for both entities for her exemplary service to the community.

Angela's mantra is *"My Words Have POWER!"* Since its inception in January 2015, PGP has been blessed with an ever-growing and diverse group of almost 100 authors who have penned topics related to faith, love, abuse, bullying, Bible study tools, marriage, and so much more. Their youngest author is only two years old; their eldest is 75 years old at the time of this publication. To their credit and God's glory, PGP and RSP have collectively over 150 best-selling titles to date.

An affordable publishing option (in comparison to some of the large, traditional publishing houses), PGP and RSP work one-on-one with authors to ensure that financial hardship is not a discouraging part of the publishing process. For those desiring to share their God-inspired messages for the masses, to include both new and 'seasoned' authors, both publishing houses provide unique services and support that many have said "left them feeling as if they are the only author" placed under each company's care.

The Holy Bible states that "God loves a cheerful giver" (2 Corinthians 9:7). To that end, PGP and RSP are frequently found hosting fantastic giveaways. Throughout the past few years, new author contests have awarded authors over $12,000.00 in services total.

In addition to the aforementioned, Angela is a domestic abuse survivor. Since first telling her abuse-survivor story publicly, she has become a 'Trumpet for Change.' She established the **"Battle-Scar Free Movement"** — an online community of individuals who freely express and share their own overcoming-testimonies while, at the same time, begin the very necessary healing process of the heart, mind, and soul. As part of her God-given mission, she provides abuse victims and survivors a **FREE** opportunity to anonymously share their testimonies in a book series entitled *God Says I am Battle-Scar Free*. Although the series will be completed in the Spring of

2021, Angela's mission to help individuals heal with the power of their words will continue. Assisting others with the healing process is paramount to her, which propelled her into becoming a volunteer Mentor for the Star of Hope Mission in Houston, Texas.

Angela holds an A.A. Degree in Business Administration from the University of Phoenix and is working towards her B.S. Degree in Psychology with a concentration in Christian Counseling from LeTourneau University. She is a woman of God, wife, mother, grandmother of 12, and trusted friend. Originally a New Jersey native, she has since made Texas her home and embraced the southern culture in all of its fullness. She loves life and affirms daily: **"NOT TODAY, SATAN!"**

Compiled by Angela R. Edwards

Contact the Publisher

Pearly Gates Publishing and Redemption's Story Publishing are always looking for new talent and desires to "birth the writer" in **YOU**! Will *YOU* be next on their list of Best-Selling Authors?

Contact us today!

Visit PGP on the Web at www.PearlyGatesPublishing.com

Visit RSP on the Web at www.Redemptions-Story.com

Connect with PGP on Facebook at
www.facebook.com/pearlygatespublishing

Connect with RSP on Facebook at
www.facebook.com/RedemptionsStoryPublishing

Email Angela Edwards, CEO at
pearlygatespublishing@gmail.com

Call 1-833-PGP-BOOK(s)
to schedule your **FREE** 15-minute publishing consultation.

www.ingramcontent.com/pod-product-compliance
Lightning Source LLC
Chambersburg PA
CBHW052159110526
44591CB00012B/2001